PREHISTORIC PREDATORS

BRIAN SWITEK • ILLUSTRATED BY JULIUS CSOTONYI

APPLESAUCE PRESS

Kennebunkport, ME

13-Digit ISBN: 978-1604335521
10-Digit ISBN: 1604335521

This book may be ordered by mail from the publisher. Please include $4.95 for postage and handling.
Please support your local bookseller first!

Books published by Cider Mill Press Book Publishers are available at special discounts
for bulk purchases in the United States by corporations, institutions, and other organizations.
For more information, please contact the publisher.

Applesauce Press is an imprint of Cider Mill Press Book Publishers
"Where good books are ready for press"
12 Spring Street
PO Box 454
Kennebunkport, Maine 04046

Visit us on the Web!
www.cidermillpress.com

Cover and interior design by Alicia Freile, Tango Media
Layout by Gwen Galeone, Tango Media
Editing: Amy Paradysz
Typography: Gipsiero Kracxed, Imperfect, PMN Caecilia
Shutterstock images: pages 2, 8 (both), 9 (both), 34, 35, 37, 43, 52, 55, 84, 88, and 95.
All other artwork by Julius T. Csotonyi.

Printed in China

4 5 6 7 8 9 10

TABLE OF CONTENTS

INTRODUCTION

For as long as there has been life, there have been predators. For most of the last 3.8 *billion* years, those predators have been single cells that fed on other cells. Only with the origin of animals, about 600 million years ago, did things start to get really interesting. In an explosion of life, animals evolved eyes to see, limbs to grasp, mouths to crush, and other body parts that allowed them to better catch and consume prey.

But of all the predators to have ever lived, the greatest have evolved over the past 275 million years. They came in a nightmarish variety of forms. Some, such as our own protomammal cousins, had sails on their backs and mouths full of teeth like nails. They were eventually replaced by the great "ruling reptiles"—including the dinosaurs—that ranged from chicken-sized, ant-eaters like *Linhenykus* to the carnivore heralded as the greatest of all time, *Tyrannosaurus rex*. And the age of predatory prowess did not end with the extinction of the non-avian dinosaurs. In the 66 million years since an asteroid strike changed the course of life on Earth, saber-toothed cats, hell pigs, and terror birds evolved to carry on the carnivorous tradition.

These fantastic, long-lost meat-eaters hunted a variety of prey. Some, like the great *Giganotosaurus*, were the apex predators of their time, taking down prey as large as they could handle and scaring scavengers away from their kills. Others, like the pterosaur *Dsungaripterus*, specialized in crushing through the shells of invertebrates and other small morsels. And not all prehistoric predators roamed the land. The prehistoric gar *Atractosteus* snapped up unsuspecting fish in ancient lakes, while *Carcharocles megalodon*—the largest shark of all time—ripped into early whales and prehistoric seals.

We can no longer see these predators in action. The carnivores presented in these pages died out at different times in the past, long before there were any humans to see them (or be eaten by them!). All we have is what remains in the rock: bones, footprints, gut contents, and tooth marks on bone. But through paleoart—the beautiful combination of science and imagination—we can visit with these predators and envision them in their lost world. In our dreams and nightmares, prehistoric predators can live again.

Tyrannosaurus rex

CENOZOIC: 66 million years ago–present

HOLOCENE: 0.01 million years ago to present

PLEISTOCENE: 2.6–0.01 million years ago

PLIOCENE: 5.3–2.6 million years ago

MIOCENE: 23–5.3 million years ago

OLIGOCENE: 33.9–23 million years ago

EOCENE: 56–33.9 million years ago

PALEOCENE: 66–56 million years ago

CRETACEOUS: 145–66 million years ago

JURASSIC: 201–145 million years ago

TRIASSIC: 252–201 million years ago

PERMIAN: 299–252 million years ago

PERMIAN
PERIOD
299–252 MILLION YEARS AGO

As the sun rises in prehistoric Texas, 275 million years ago, predators set about getting their breakfast. While a sail-backed Dimetrodon nabs the shark Xenacanthus (far right) the giant amphibian Eryops makes off with a boomerang-headed Diplocaulus (far left).

As dawn broke on the first day of the Permian period, about 299 million years ago, the sunlight greeted a world very different from the one we know today. All of the world's continents had drifted into each other to create one supercontinent—Pangaea—surrounded by a vast, warm global ocean called Panthalassa. And for the next 47 million years, our distant cousins and ancestors were the dominant predators on the planet.

Early in the Permian, our ancestors looked like little lizards. From the outside, it would be hard to tell the difference between your great-great-great-great-and a bunch more great-grandma and a gecko you might see at the pet store. But if you could look at the skull of one of these little critters, you would be able to see something that connects you to those lizard-like creatures of the Permian. These animals had a single opening at the back of their skull—a trait that marks the lizardish animals as belonging to a group called synapsids. Along with other mammals, you have a remnant of this opening in your own skull, meaning that those little "lizards" were more closely related to you than to any reptile. Because of this connection, we can say that syanpsids were protomammals.

Our protomammal relatives didn't stay small for long, though. In time, they got bigger and bigger, evolving into amazing shapes. *Dimetrodon*—a carnivore that could get up to 15 feet long and had a huge sail sticking out of its back—was one of these weird protomammals. No one knows whether the sail was useful in scaring enemies, attracting dates, storing energy to help *Dimetrodon* move, or something else. But because of that opening

Lystrosaurus

Keratocephalus

at the back of its skull, we know it was part of our bigger prehistoric family. It was just one of the first protomammal predators to rule the Permian, which later included the dog-like *Dinogorgon* and fearsome *Titanosuchus*.

But the protomammals weren't the only hunters around. From lizard-like ancestors with two openings at the back of their skulls—called diapsids—reptiles started to flourish, too, including carnivores like *Archosaurus*. This hook-snouted, snaggle-toothed reptile haunted waterways where it could catch protomammals by surprise when they came to get a drink.

While such reptilian carnivores were rare compared to their protomammal counterparts, a terrible catastrophe at the end of the Permian period would clear their path to start the Age of Reptiles.

Estemmenosuchus

Fragmentary fossil of Dimetrodon

A lone Dimetrodon *is silhouetted against the morning sky. Paleontologists used to think that the protomammal turned its big sail toward the sun to help it warm up each morning. But newer evidence suggests that those long spines and the skin between them evolved as a display structure. Such a big, flashy ornament would have helped these predators figure out who was who as they walked across the Permian landscape, and* Dimetrodon *may have even used the sails as biological billboards to show off during the mating season.*

DIMETRODON
LIMBATUS

PRONUNCIATION: DY-met-RO-don

SIZE: Up to 15 feet long

AGE: 295–272 million years ago.

PHYSICAL PROFILE: A squat, four-legged carnivore that sported a huge, thin sail along its back.

SCIENCE BITE: Even though *Dimetrodon* was a protomammal relative of ours, they still reproduced by laying eggs. And baby *Dimetrodon* had tiny sails on their backs like their parents!

DINOGORGON
RUBIDGEI

PRONUNCIATION: DY-no-GORE-gon

SIZE: About 6 feet long

AGE: 252 million years ago

PHYSICAL PROFILE: A hunter that ran on all fours and dispatched prey with long, pointed canine teeth.

SCIENCE BITE: *Dinogorgon* was one of the last great predatory protomammals, living right before the world's worst mass extinction removed them from dominance.

Of all the Permian protomammals, the gorgonopsids were among the fiercest predators. Some of the largest, such as these dueling Dinogorgon, grew to the size of a black bear and they dispatched prey with their long, stabbing saber teeth. More than that, the gorgonopsids were faster than earlier Permian carnivores. While predators like Dimetrodon had legs splayed out to their sides like lizards, Dinogorgon and its deadly kin had legs held more upright, toward the middle of the body, and this made them quicker, more efficient pursuit predators.

TITANOSUCHUS FEROX

PRONUNCIATION: TIE-tan-O-sook-US

SIZE: Up to 9 feet long

AGE: About 265 million years ago

PHYSICAL PROFILE: A protomammal that walked on four legs and had a long skull of pointed teeth that differed in shape from front to back.

SCIENCE BITE: Instead of scaly skin, *Titanosuchus* had smooth skin that may have been partly covered in hair.

The Permian was a protomammal-eat-protomammal world. Here a Titanosuchus ambushes a Moschops, a bulky herbivore that shared the same habitats in prehistoric South Africa. Both predator and prey are distant cousins of ours, more closely related to mammals than any reptile. And despite its plain appearance, Moschops had an extraordinary skull. The domed head of Moschops was reinforced with very thick bone. No one yet knows the reason why, but paleontologists hypothesize that Moschops might have fought each other by butting heads!

ARCHOSAURUS ROSSICUS

PRONUNCIATION: ARK-uh-SAWR-us

SIZE: About 10 feet long

AGE: Around 252 million years ago

PHYSICAL PROFILE: *Archosaurus* hunted prey on all fours and had a downward-kinked snout that gave it a snaggle-toothed look.

SCIENCE BITE: *Archosaurus* was one of the largest reptilian predators of its time, setting the stage for its relatives to become even bigger during the Triassic period.

TRIASSIC

252–201 MILLION YEARS AGO

About 252 million years ago—which paleontologists mark as the end of the Permian period—life on Earth suffered the worst catastrophe of all time. More than 95 percent of species in the seas disappeared, as well as 75 percent of species on land. Only a scant few survivors of the Permian world were left, among them reptiles that would outcompete the remaining protomammals to become some of the strangest and most magnificent carnivores of all time.

These reptilian survivors began to flourish during the Triassic, which stretched from 252 to 200 million years ago. Of these, the most successful belonged to a group called the Archosauria, the "ruling reptiles." They included the ancestors of crocodiles, flying pterosaurs, and, most famous of all, dinosaurs. By about 245 million years ago—only 7 million years after the mass extinction—all of these groups had split from each other and began to evolve in startling new ways.

Dinosaurs weren't dominant right from the start, though. Little *Eoraptor*, only about as big as a turkey, was an omnivore. The leaf-shaped teeth in this early dinosaur's jaw indicate that it ate plants as well as chasing down small prey such as insects and tiny mammals. The most formidable Triassic predators were different sorts of carnivores.

EORAPTOR
LUNENSIS

PRONUNCIATION: EE-o-RAP-tor

SIZE: About 3 feet long

AGE: About 231 million years ago

PHYSICAL PROFILE: One of the earliest known dinosaurs, *Eoraptor* was a bipedal animal with leaf-shaped teeth.

SCIENCE BITE: *Eoraptor* wasn't the only hunter in its habitat. It lived alongside the sharp-toothed *Herrerasaurus*, which could grow up to 10 feet long.

With a deep skull set with knife-like teeth and the ability to walk on two legs, Postosuchus might look like a dinosaur. But, because of the anatomy of its hips and ankles, paleontologists know that this monstrous predator was actually a closer relative to the earliest crocodiles. During a time when dinosaurs were rare and small, croc-cousins like Postosuchus were the true rulers of the Triassic world.

POSTOSUCHUS
KIRKPATRICKI

PRONUNCIATION: POST-o-SOOK-us

SIZE: Up to 16 feet long

AGE: Between 228 and 202 million years ago

PHYSICAL PROFILE: A bulky predator with strong legs, small arms, and a deep skull capable of delivering a crushing bite.

SCIENCE BITE: Damaged armor plates found in Triassic rock suggest that predators like Postosuchus were capable of literally cracking the defenses of their victims.

During Triassic time, crocodile cousins ruled. Here, near the edge of an immense conifer forest that once covered eastern Arizona, a highly armored Desmatosuchus tries to fend off a rapacious Postosuchus. The herbivore's body armor certainly give it a fighting chance. Those plates and spikes are made of bone embedded in the skin. Paleontologists call them osteoderms—skin bones—and have found some relatives of Desmatosuchus with parts of their armor still in place after more than 220 million years.

The most common carnivores of all were the phytosaurs, like *Smilosuchus*. They looked like the crocodiles we know today and lived much the same way, but they actually belonged to an older, more archaic group. One way to tell is by looking at the placement of their nostrils—on the tops of their skulls, near the eyes, rather than at the front. They were living the crocodile life before there were actual crocodiles, launching themselves after prey from the water's edge. Along with the likes of *Postosuchus* and early dinosaurs, they made the Triassic a very dangerous time to be alive.

SMILOSUCHUS GREGORII

PRONUNCIATION: SMILE-o-SOOK-us

SIZE: Up to 15 feet long

AGE: About 228 million years ago

PHYSICAL PROFILE: A large phytosaur, *Smilosuchus* looked like a crocodile but had nostrils far back on its snout, near the eyes.

SCIENCE BITE: Paleontologists have found a leg bone of another Triassic predator with a phytosaur tooth marks surrounded by healed bone, meaning the animal escaped a close call with a carnivore like *Smilosuchus*.

Going down to the water for a drink was risky business during the Late Triassic. The lakes and rivers of the time were home to phytosaurs—crocodile-like carnivores that hid beneath the surface until prey got close enough to strike. And thanks to some bitten Triassic bones, paleontologists know that phytosaurs sometimes ate protomammals such as this unlucky Placerias. A tusked, tubby herbivore, Placerias was one of the last surviving members of a protomammal group called dicynodonts. These beaked plant-eaters were frequently food for the carnivores they lived alongside.

JURASSIC
PERIOD
201–145 MILLION YEARS AGO

Even though dinosaurs had been around since early in the Triassic period, the Jurassic period was truly the beginning of the Age of Dinosaurs. That's because dinosaurs were lucky. Another mass extinction at the end of the Triassic wiped out most of the crocodile cousins that had been the largest and most numerous creatures of the age, but did not seem to harm the dinosaurs at all. The world was ready for dinosaur dominance.

A large part of this dinosaur success story is told through their range in size. During the Jurassic, predatory dinosaurs—all of them belonging to a subgroup called theropods—ranged from the pigeon-sized *Anchiornis* to hypercarnivores that could reach lengths of 40 feet, as we know from some rare specimens of *Allosaurus*. Dinosaurs filled the Jurassic world with a stunning variety of shapes and sizes.

And many of these Jurassic theropods were flashy predators. One of the earliest, the slender and agile *Dilophosaurus*, had a pair of thin crests running along its head. Its cousin *Cryolophosaurus* showed off in a different way, with a cockscomb sticking up over its eyes, and the later, even bigger *Allosaurus* had a triangular horn over each eye. No one knows exactly why these predators had these ornaments. They were too delicate to be weapons, but they may have helped these dinosaurs recognize their own kind at a distance or impress potential mates.

ALLOSAURUS FRAGILIS

PRONUNCIATION: AL-uh-SAWR-us

SIZE: Up to 30 feet long and 1 ton

AGE: 150–148 million years ago

PHYSICAL PROFILE: Big predator that grappled prey with strong, three-clawed arms and snapped at flesh with a light, slender skull.

SCIENCE BITE: *Allosaurus* probably fed like falcons do today, pinning carcasses with its feet and ripping off chunks of flesh with powerful jerks of its neck.

ost of what we know about *Dilophosaurus* comes from the dinosaur's bones. But there's another kind of evidence paleontologists can study to learn about dinosaur lives: trace fossils. These are tracks and other traces that reflect prehistoric behavior. And at one site in southern Utah, paleontologists have uncovered a spot where a *Dilophosaurus*—or very similar dinosaur—laid down for a rest. The mark in the rock shows marks from the dinosaur's tail, hip, feet, and hands as it sat by the side of a lake, eventually shuffling forward and walking off along the shore. This trace is the closest we can get to watching a living *Dilophosaurus*.

DILOPHOSAURUS WETHERILLI

PRONUNCIATION: DY-low-pho-SAWR-us

SIZE: About 23 feet long and 1,000 pounds

AGE: About 193 million years ago

PHYSICAL PROFILE: A slender, medium-sized predator immediately recognizable by the thin, paired crests on top of its head.

SCIENCE BITE: *Dilophosaurus* didn't have a neck frill or spit venom like in *Jurassic Park*. The dinosaur's teeth and jaws were enough to subdue its victims.

26

We often think of tyrannosaurs as giant carnivores with huge heads and tiny arms. Back in the Jurassic period, however, tyrannosaurs were small predators with very different proportions. One of the earliest was Guanlong—a tyrant dinosaur with long arms, a shallow snout, a prominent crest on its head, and a coat of dinofuzz on its body. Guanlong and its early tyrannosaur relatives elsewhere eked out a living in environments patrolled by much bigger allosaurs and other predators, and it was only much later, during the Cretaceous period, that tyrannosaurs got large enough to rule.

GUANLONG WUCAII

PRONUNCIATION: GWAN-long

SIZE: Almost 10 feet long

AGE: About 160 million years ago

PHYSICAL PROFILE: A small tyrannosaur with long arms, a shallow skull, and a prominent crest jutting from its face.

SCIENCE BITE: The first skeleton of *Guanlong* was found in a weird deathtrap—a huge mudhole made by the footprint of a long-necked sauropod dinosaur.

The bones of Cryolophosaurus *were found in what might seem like a very unusual place for a dinosaur: Antarctica. Today, the cold, rocky exposures where the fossils were found are inhospitable, but during the Jurassic period the same land was much closer to the equator. The weather back then could still get a little cool, but Jurassic Antarctica was much warmer than the continent is today, hosting lush forests where* Cryolophosaurus *and big, long-necked sauropod dinosaurs such as* Glacialisaurus *roamed.*

CRYOLOPHOSAURUS ELLIOTI

PRONUNCIATION: CRY-uh-LOW-pho-SAWR-us

SIZE: About 21 feet long and 1,000 pounds

AGE: About 190 million years ago

PHYSICAL PROFILE: A mid-size carnivore with a deep skull, three-clawed hands, and a ridged crest atop its head.

SCIENCE BITE: The paleontologists who discovered *Cryolophosaurus* were so impressed with its bony pompadour that they nicknamed the animal "Elvisaurus."

During the Jurassic, dinosaurs were getting fluffy and fuzzy. Dinofuzz—the wispy precursors to true feathers—were a common feature of carnivorous dinosaurs. This prehistoric fluff helped keep dinosaurs warm and was also useful in display.

Some lineages even evolved ever-more complex plumage that allowed dinosaurs to take to the air. In fact, thanks to beautifully preserved dinosaurs like *Anchiornis*, paleontologists know that birds—including every bird alive today—are really predatory dinosaurs. The first birds evolved about 150 million years ago, late in the Jurassic, and lived alongside the rest of their dinosaurian family until another extinction at the end of the Cretaceous period wiped out all the non-bird dinosaurs. So when you look at a bird today—whether it's a penguin or a pigeon—you're seeing the descendants of feathery dinosaurs that learned to fly way back in the Jurassic period!

ANCHIORNIS HUXLEYI

PRONUNCIATION: ANK-ee-OR-niss

SIZE: A foot long, about the size of a common crow

AGE: About 160 million years ago

PHYSICAL PROFILE: With long arms, a little sickle claw on each foot, and tiny teeth, the feathery *Anchiornis* fluttered after insects and other small prey.

SCIENCE BITE: Despite its feathers, *Anchiornis* was not a skilled flyer yet. It could flutter and glide but not sustain flight like modern birds can.

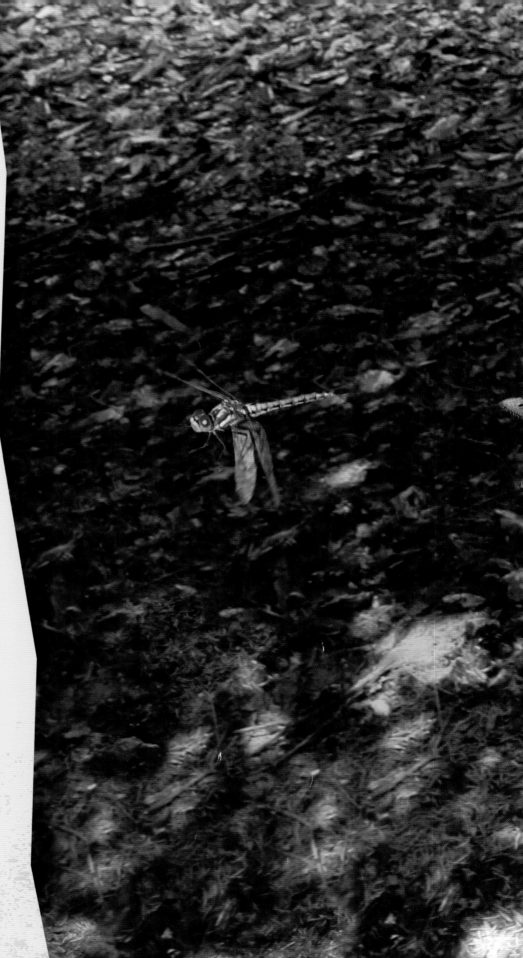

For most dinosaurs, we don't know what colors they really were. Anchiornis *is* an exception. Paleontologists have been able to work out this little dinosaur's plumage palette thanks to its feathers. Just like modern birds, Anchiornis *had colors created by tiny structures on its feathers called melanosomes. And because these structures make colors, paleontologists have been able to compare the feathers of* Anchiornis *with those of living birds. They found that* Anchiornis *was mostly black with white patches on its wings and a splash of red on its head. This made the dinosaur look like a punk rock magpie, complete with teeth and claws.*

CRETACEOUS

PERIOD

145–66 MILLION YEARS AGO

The Jurassic period was only the beginning of dinosaur dominance. The Cretaceous period was a long continuation of their reign, stretching from 145 to 66 million years ago. Just think about how much time that is. The Cretaceous lasted for 79 million years, but there have only been 66 million years between us and the very last *Tyrannosaurus rex*. You could fit the entire "Age of Mammals" into just the Cretaceous part of the dinosaur rule with plenty of time to spare. Dinosaurs and the other forms of life they lived alongside didn't stay static, though. As the continents continued to shift and the climate changed, life on Earth evolved into amazing—and sometimes frightening!—new forms.

Consider the truly giant carnivorous dinosaurs— the ones that reached 40 feet long or more. One of the earliest was *Acrocanthosaurus*, a 110 million-year-old cousin of the earlier *Allosaurus* that roamed prehistoric North America with hooked hand claws, knife-like teeth, and a strange ridge running the length of its back. At around the same time, but in Africa, there lived an even stranger sail-backed predator: *Spinosaurus*. This giant had a long snout brimming with rounded teeth suited to catching fish and other slippery prey, although this dinosaur's most fetching feature was a seven-foot-tall sail growing up from its spine. Later dinosaurian predators included *Giganotosaurus*—a 97 million-year-old relative of *Acrocanthosaurus*— and, of course, the great *Tyrannosaurus* from between 68 and 66 million years ago. Over and over again, the Cretaceous saw the evolution of flesh-ripping giants.

But the Cretaceous also saw the rise of smaller predators that relied more on claws than jaws. These were the fast, feathery "raptor" dinosaurs like *Velociraptor* and *Troodon*. Paleontologists know them as deinonychosaurs—the "terrible-clawed reptiles"—and they were immediately recognizable by a modified second toe on each foot that was held off the ground and bore a large, curved killing claw. How these dinosaurs used the claw is a paleo puzzle, but, given their size, it's likely that dinosaurs like *Velociraptor* used their claws like hawks and falcons do today. The raptors pounced on smaller dinosaurs and mammals, pinning their victims down with their toe claw while flapping their feathery arms. And raptor foot impressions found with mammal burrows hint that some of these smaller predators clawed into the soil to dig our mammalian relatives out of their dens.

Of course, dinosaur dominance eventually came to an end. A combination of climate change, intense volcanic activity, and a massive asteroid impact set off another mass extinction 66 million years ago. Many forms of Cretaceous life perished—in the seas as well as on land—and not a single non-avian dinosaur survived. Birds were the only dinosaurs to carry on their family's legacy into the next chapter of Earth's story.

VELOCIRAPTOR MONGOLIENSIS

PRONUNCIATION: VEL-oss-EE-RAP-tor

SIZE: Turkey-size, or about 7 feet long with the tail

AGE: Between 75 and 71 million years ago

PHYSICAL PROFILE: An iconic "raptor" with grasping hands, stiff tail, and an extendable toe tipped with a large claw on the inside of each foot.

SCIENCE BITE: *Velociraptor* didn't only hunt. Damaged bones in their gut contents have shown these dinosaurs would scavenge when they got the chance.

Dinosaurs were hardly the only carnivores of the Mesozoic period. Their cousins, the pterosaurs, were also major predators of the age. These flying reptiles soared through the air on wings of skin extended on extremely long fourth fingers, and many were covered by a coat of insulating fuzz. The last of the pterosaurs had pointed, toothless beaks, but there were also many forms that had teeth suited to different diets. While some pterosaurs had pointed teeth useful for trapping insects and small fish, for example, species like this Dsungaripterus had flat crushing teeth specialized for cracking the shells of invertebrates, like this coil-shelled squid cousin called an ammonite.

DSUNGARIPTERUS WEII

PRONUNCIATION: JUNG-gar-IP-ter-us

SIZE: A wingspan of almost 10 feet

AGE: About 130 million years ago

PHYSICAL PROFILE: This pterosaur had a low crest running down the top of its skull and an upturned, toothy beak.

SCIENCE BITE: *Dsungaripterus* and other pterosaurs took off with a pole-vault move, pushing off the ground with their arms and throwing their wings open to start flapping into the air.

Ammonites, ancient cousins of octopus and squid, lived inside coiled shells.

MICRORAPTOR GUI

PRONUNCIATION: MY-crow-RAP-tor

SIZE: Up to 4 feet long

AGE: Between 125 and 120 million years ago

PHYSICAL PROFILE: This raven-sized dinosaur had long feathers on its arms, legs, and at the end of its tail, which allowed it to fly in a way unlike birds today.

SCIENCE BITE: Gut contents in *Microraptor* skeletons have shown that this dinosaur often ate small prey such as shrew-like mammals and early birds.

SINORNITHOSAURUS MILLENII

PRONUNCIATION: SINE-or-NITH-o-SAWR-us

SIZE: About 3 feet long

AGE: About 124 million years ago

PHYSICAL PROFILE: A small "raptor" dinosaur, covered in feathers, with a highly extendable claw on each foot.

SCIENCE BITE: From the anatomy of its eyes, paleontologists expect that *Sinornithosaurus* hunted from dawn to dusk at short intervals.

Just like many habitats today, prehistoric environments often hosted an array of different predators. Here, the bulldog-faced dinosaur Kryptops (left) takes a drink while the long-snouted Suchomimus (right) grabs a baby Sarcosuchus—a crocodile that could grow up to 40 feet long if it survived to adulthood. Predators such as these were able to coexist because they targeted different prey and fed in different ways. While big Sarcosuchus lurked in the water, Suchomimus hunted among both the lakes and the land, and Kryptops targeted smaller prey on shore. Every predator had their own set of hunting skills, and that's what allowed so many forms to stalk the same habitats.

SUCHOMIMUS
TENERENSIS

PRONUNCIATION: SOOK-o-MIME-us

SIZE: About 30 feet long

AGE: Between 121 and 113 million years ago

PHYSICAL PROFILE: A large predatory dinosaur with thick, grasping claws on the hands, a low sail on its back, and a very long snout that gave this "crocodile mimic" its name.

SCIENCE BITE: No one knows why *Suchomimus* had a sail on its back. If you grow up to be a paleontologist, maybe you'll find out!

KRYPTOPS PALAIOS

PRONUNCIATION: CRYP-tops

SIZE: About 20 feet long

AGE: 110 million years ago

PHYSICAL PROFILE: This stout carnivore had small, weak arms and a short, deep skull that gave it a bulldog-like appearance.

SCIENCE BITE: Based on the blood vessels and grooves on the upper jaw bones, paleontologists suspect that *Kryptops* had some kind of tough, rough facial covering.

During the early part of the Cretaceous, cousins of Allosaurus were the biggest, baddest carnivores around. Among the most imposing was Acrocanthosaurus, and a curious trackway found in Texas might even show this predator in action. The main trackway preserves the pothole-like footsteps of a long-necked, heavy-bodied sauropod dinosaur. The tracks of a very large predator—likely Acrocanthosaurus or a close relative—come in from the side and collide with those of the giant herbivore. What does this mean? Perhaps the Acrocanthosaurus was stalking its prey from a distance, following it until just the right moment. Or maybe the tracks record an attack. Some paleontologists point to a missing Acrocanthosaurus track as the moment when the carnivore bit the sauropod and was lifted off its feet. Either way, being followed by an Acrocanthosaurus must have been a chilling experience.

ACROCANTHOSAURUS ATOKENSIS

PRONUNCIATION: AK-ro-KANTH-uh-SAWR-us

SIZE: Up to 40 feet long and 6 tons

AGE: About 110 million years ago

PHYSICAL PROFILE: Huge carnivore with a large skull set with knife-like teeth, three-clawed arms, and a high, prominent ridge running along its back.

SCIENCE BITE: Acrocanthosaurus arm anatomy suggests this carnivore could dig its large claws into prey and hold victims close while delivering a fatal bite. In other words, its hugs were deadly.

DELTADROMEUS AGILIS

PRONUNCIATION: DEL-ta-DRO-me-us

SIZE: About 26 feet long

AGE: Around 95 million years ago

PHYSICAL PROFILE: A medium-sized, slender carnivore with long legs for its size.

SCIENCE BITE: *Deltadromeus* had stiff competition for food, as it lived in the same place and at the same time as the bigger predators *Spinosaurus*, *Carcharodontosaurus*, and *Bahariasaurus*.

SPINOSAURUS
AEGYPTIACUS

PRONUNCIATION: SPY-no-SAWR-us

SIZE: About 45 feet long

AGE: Between 112 and 97 million years ago

PHYSICAL PROFILE: A huge, sail-backed carnivore with a long, low skull full of conical teeth.

SCIENCE BITE: *Spinosaurus* had very dense bones, which may have acted like ballast to help keep the dinosaur submerged when it went hunting in lakes and rivers.

GIGANOTOSAURUS CAROLINII

PRONUNCIATION:
JIG-an-O-to-SAWR-us

SIZE: Up to 40 feet long and 13 tons

AGE: Between 100 and 97 million years ago

PHYSICAL PROFILE: A giant, heavily built carnivore with a long, deep skull fitted with flattened, blade-like teeth.

EKRIXINATOSAURUS NOVASI

PRONUNCIATION: EK-rix-IN-at-o-SAWR-us

SIZE: About 25 feet long

AGE: Between 100 and 97 million years ago

PHYSICAL PROFILE: Large carnivore with a short, deep skull and tiny arms.

SCIENCE BITE: Why *Ekrixinatosaurus* and its close relatives had such small arms is a mystery, but the muscle attachments on their bones hint that they were still useful for *something*.

EOCARCHARIA DINOPS

PRONUNCIATION: EE-o-CAR-char-EE-ah

SIZE: About 25 feet long

AGE: 110 million years ago

PHYSICAL PROFILE: A mid-sized predator with a long, deep skull full of knife-shaped teeth that give this "dawn shark" dinosaur its name.

SCIENCE BITE: A rough ridge of bone on this dinosaur's brow is why paleontologists gave it the species name *dinops*, meaning "fierce-eyed."

LINHENYKUS
MONODACTYLUS

PRONUNCIATION: LIN-heh-NYE-cuss

SIZE: About 3 feet long

AGE: Between 84 and 75 million years ago

PHYSICAL PROFILE: This tiny dinosaur had a small skull with toothless jaws and short, stubby arms tipped with a single clawed finger each.

SCIENCE BITE: *Linhenykus* didn't just have short arms. This little dinosaur only had one finger on each hand!

The anatomy of prehistoric predators doesn't only reflect what that animal was eating. It can also help paleontologists identify some major events in the history of life on Earth. Linhenykus and its close relatives were small dinosaurs with short, stout hand claws and few or no teeth in their mouths. Because of this, paleontologists think they were the dinosaur equivalents of anteaters. Paleontologists have found termite nests in petrified wood going back to the Jurassic period. Other social insects like bees were evolving in the early Cretaceous period, so it's no surprise that some dinosaurs evolved to exploit this new source of crunchy insect food!

LINHERAPTOR EXQUISITUS

PRONUNCIATION: LIN-heh-RAP-tor

SIZE: Almost 7 feet long

AGE: Between 84 and 75 million years ago

PHYSICAL PROFILE: A mid-sized "raptor" dinosaur, with large, grasping hands, a stiff tail, and an extendable claw on each foot suited to pinning down prey.

SCIENCE BITE: Even though no feathers were found with the skeleton, we know from close relatives that *Linheraptor* was definitely a fluffy dinosaur.

Many dinosaurs, like Linheraptor, were covered with feathers. That might seem strange for animals that couldn't fly, but paleontologists have found that feathers first evolved for reasons other than taking to the air. Starting with wisps of fluff and fuzz, the earliest feathers helped keep dinosaurs warm. This was especially important for little dinosaurs, who had a harder time keeping warm on prehistoric nights. And paleontologists have also discovered that feathered dinosaurs often had unique color patterns and feather shapes that wouldn't have been useful for flying but would have been great for display. Over time, there were even more uses for dinosaur feathers. Predators like Linheraptor could have flapped their feathery arms to help them keep a grip on titled surfaces like fallen logs or to help keep pinned-down prey from escaping.

OVIRAPTOR
PHILOCERATOPS

PRONUNCIATION: OH-vee-RAP-tor

SIZE: About 5 feet long

AGE: Around 75 million years ago

PHYSICAL PROFILE: A dinosaur that walked on two legs with a covering of feathers and a toothless, parrot-like beak.

SCIENCE BITE: Even though its name means "egg thief," *Oviraptor* were good parents. Some *Oviraptor* died while brooding their eggs to keep them warm.

Not all predatory dinosaurs had big, sharp teeth. The parrot-like Oviraptor did not have a tooth in its mouth, yet it was capable of eating a mixed diet of both greens and meat. Like most other dinosaurs, Oviraptor couldn't chew. Some bones jutting down from the roof of its mouth could have helped it crush small morsels, but, beyond that, Oviraptor had to swallow each mouthful whole. Fortunately for this dinosaur, there were plenty of appetizers in its Cretaceous habitat. Paleontologists have found freshwater clams in the same area as Oviraptor, which the dinosaur could have cracked open in its beak, and one specimen of the predator was found with a small lizard inside. It just goes to show that the Age of Dinosaurs was a time of small predators as well as huge ones.

Dinosaurs are often ridiculed for having brains "the size of a walnut," but this wasn't true of all species. For its size, Troodon actually had a relatively large brain. Paleontologists can tell this from the inside of its skull. Dinosaur brains fit relatively tightly in the bone of the skull, and so the inside of dinosaur skulls preserve what's called a brain endocast. By making molds and 3D models of this cavity, paleontologists can get a good idea of the size and shape of dinosaur brains. In the case of Troodon, the dinosaur's brain was more than five times larger than expected for a dinosaur of its size. Combined with the fact that Troodon had forward-facing eyes—giving it binocular vision like we have—paleontologists expect that this dinosaur was a very clever little hunter with the ability to quickly pinpoint scurrying mammals and other small prey. Telling how smart Troodon was is another matter, but, based on what we know about its living relatives, the dinosaur may have been as intelligent as a raven or crow.

TROODON FORMOSUS

PRONUNCIATION: TRO-o-DON

SIZE: Almost 8 feet long

AGE: About 77 million years ago

PHYSICAL PROFILE: A slender "raptor" dinosaur, with small teeth, large eyes, and an extendable toe claw on each foot.

SCIENCE BITE: *Troodon* moms laid eggs, but paleontologists have found that the dads were the ones who sat on the nest.

GORGOSAURUS LIBRATUS

PRONUNCIATION: GORE-go-SAWR-us

SIZE: Up to 30 feet long

AGE: Between 76 and 75 million years ago

PHYSICAL PROFILE: A sleek, agile tyrannosaur with a shallow skull and small horns above the eyes.

SCIENCE BITE: Young *Gorgosaurus* could pack on the pounds. During their adolescence, *Gorgosaurus* could gain over 110 pounds each year!

Prehistoric predators took their meals where they could find them. In many cases, that meant running down their dinner. This Gorgosaurus, for example, had a light build and long legs that made it a very agile hunter, able to outmaneuver some of the herbivorous dinosaurs of its time. But carnivores regularly scavenged, too. Thanks to its well-developed sense of smell, Gorgosaurus was able to sniff out rotting carcasses—like this decaying Xiphactinus fish—as well as live prey. Tyrannosaurs like Gorgosaurus were not exclusively hunters or scavengers. They certainly did both to keep their strength up.

DASPLETOSAURUS
TOROSUS

PRONUNCIATION: DAS-pleet-uh-SAWR-us

SIZE: Up to 30 feet long and 2.7 tons

AGE: 77 to 74 million years ago

PHYSICAL PROFILE: A big, heavily built tyrannosaur with a more powerful bite than its neighbor *Gorgosaurus*.

SCIENCE BITE: Some *Daspletosaurus* skulls have healed bite wounds made by other tyrannosaurs. When these dinosaurs fought, they went right for the face!

Daspletosaurus and its tyrannosaur relatives were some of the largest and most impressive predators of the Cretaceous period. So why did they have such small arms? Paleontologists have been puzzling over that mystery since the first good skeletons of tyrannosaurs were discovered in the early 20th century. One early idea was that tyrannosaurs used their tiny arms to hold onto their mates, and another popular guess was that tyrannosaurs used their arms to push themselves off the ground after napping. But neither idea explained why their arms seem so much smaller than those of their ancestors. That has more to do with the way tyrannosaurs changed their hunting strategy. Small, early tyrannosaurs used their arms to grasp prey, but as tyrannosaurs got larger and starting using their jaws to kill and rip apart prey, their skulls evolved to be bigger and carry heavier, stronger muscles. As this happened, their arms became smaller and smaller to prevent the dinosaurs from being front-heavy and falling on their faces. This trade-off let tyrannosaurs evolve some of the most powerful jaws of all time, and, although quite small, their arms still had some pretty strong muscles. That's the new mystery paleontologists face. *Daspletosaurus* and other tyrannosaurs were doing something with those little arms, but what?

CARNOTAURUS
SASTREI

PRONUNCIATION: CAR-no-TAUR-us

SIZE: About 30 feet long

AGE: Between 72 and 69 million years ago

PHYSICAL PROFILE: A large carnivore with stubby arms and a deep skull bearing a short triangular horn projecting over each eye.

SCIENCE BITE: Skin impressions found with one specimen indicate that *Carnotaurus* had scaly skin with rows of bigger, flattened bumps.

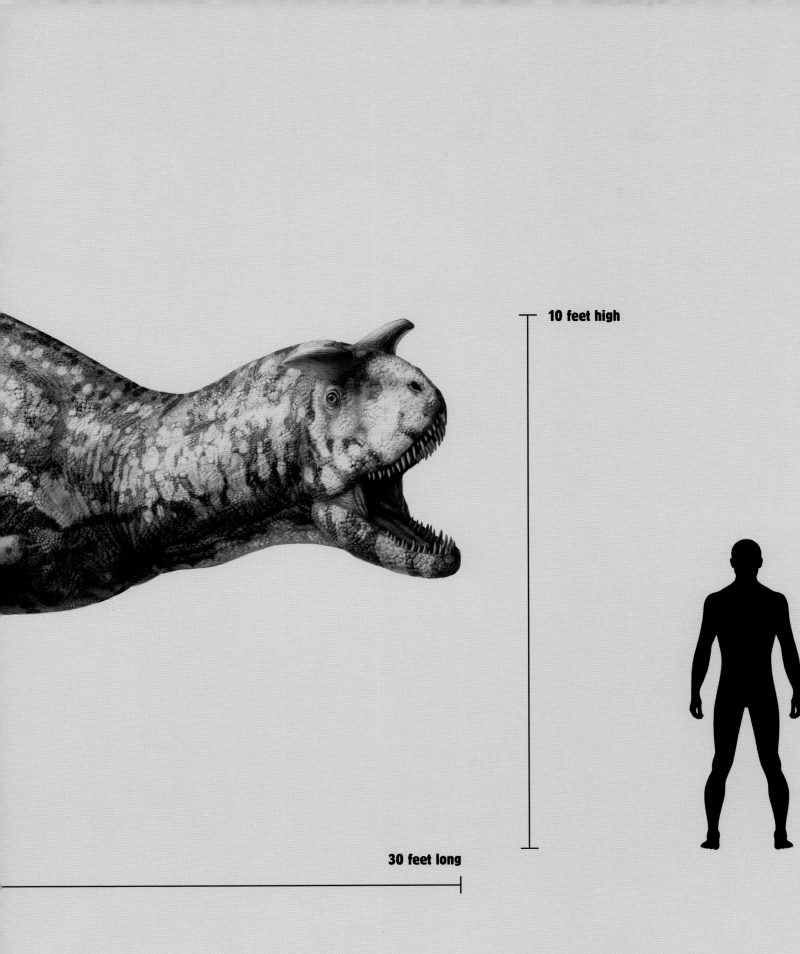

10 feet high

5 feet, 9 inches high

30 feet long

SAURORNITHOLESTES
LANGSTONI

PRONUNCIATION: SAWR-or-NITH-o-LEST-ees

SIZE: About 6 feet long

AGE: Between 77 and 70 million years ago

PHYSICAL PROFILE: A "raptor" dinosaur with grasping hands and an extendable killing claw on each foot.

SCIENCE BITE: Even predators had to watch out for bigger carnivores. One *Sauronitholestes* jaw shows bite marks from a tyrannosaur that bit the raptor on the face!

MASIAKASAURUS
KNOPFLERI

PRONUNCIATION: MA-sheek-ah-SAWR-us

SIZE: About 7 feet long

AGE: Around 70 million years ago

PHYSICAL PROFILE: A small predator with gnarly, forward-pointed teeth useful for catching fish.

SCIENCE BITE: From studies of the dinosaur's bone structure, paleontologists have figured out that it took about 10 years for *Masiakasaurus* to grow to adult size.

3 feet high

7 feet long

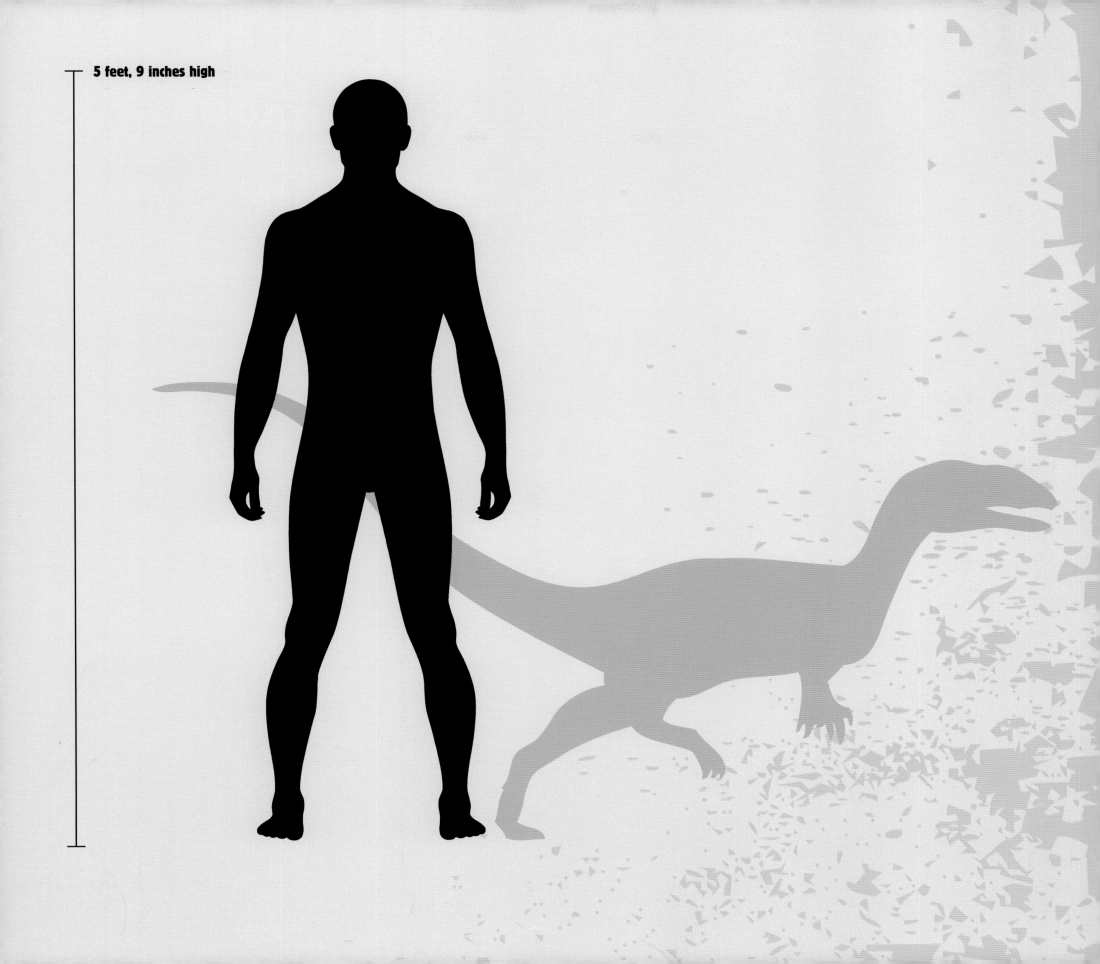

5 feet, 9 inches high

ALBERTOSAURUS SARCOPHAGUS

PRONUNCIATION: al-BER-tuh-SAWR-us

SIZE: Up to 30 feet long and 1.9 tons

AGE: 70 million years ago

PHYSICAL PROFILE: A large, sleek tyrannosaur with a big skull and tiny arms but more agility than the beefier *T. rex*.

SCIENCE BITE: In Alberta, Canada, paleontologists have found at least 26 *Albertosaurus* in one place! No one knows exactly why so many died there, but some researchers suspect that it's a clue that *Albertosaurus* lived and hunted in packs.

Predatory dinosaurs are often shown in deadly duels with hulking herbivores. The truth is that even the biggest dinosaur carnivores probably targeted easier prey. In this case, an Albertosaurus is trying to chomp down on a baby Spinops while the infant's parent tries to drive the predator away. This was probably much more common than any showdown between Albertosaurus and full-grown Spinops. In a fight, the Albertosaurus would be much more likely to suffer injuries that could harm its ability to hunt. Infant dinosaurs, as well as those too old or sick to defend themselves, were much safer targets. In fact, this may be why infant dinosaurs are so rare in the fossil record and young dinosaurs grew quickly. Predators often picked off baby and juvenile dinosaurs, and one of the few ways to avoid becoming a snack was to grow up fast.

ORNITHOMIMUS EDMONTICUS

PRONUNCIATION: OR-nith-o-MIME-us

SIZE: About 12 feet long

AGE: Around 70 million years ago

PHYSICAL PROFILE: An ostrich-mimc dinosaur with long arms, graceful neck, and a toothless beak suited to eating plants as well as insects and small prey.

SCIENCE BITE: *Ornithomimus* was toothless, but it could have used its long arms and large claws to snatch small prey as well as pull down tree branches.

Baby dinosaurs weren't tiny copies of their parents. Dinosaurs changed dramatically as they grew up—kind of like us!—and that's true of their body coverings as well as their bones. Thanks to recent discoveries in Canada, paleontologists now know that baby *Ornithomimus* were covered with a coating of chick-like fuzz. This probably kept the little ones warm and, depending on the colors, could have provided them camouflage to hide from the likes of *Albertosaurus*. But adult *Ornithomimus* looked different. They had long feathers growing from their arms, somewhat similar to the plumes on the arms of ostriches today. Maybe the Cretaceous dinosaurs used these feathers like their modern cousins, flailing them around in mating displays and covering their nests to keep their eggs warm.

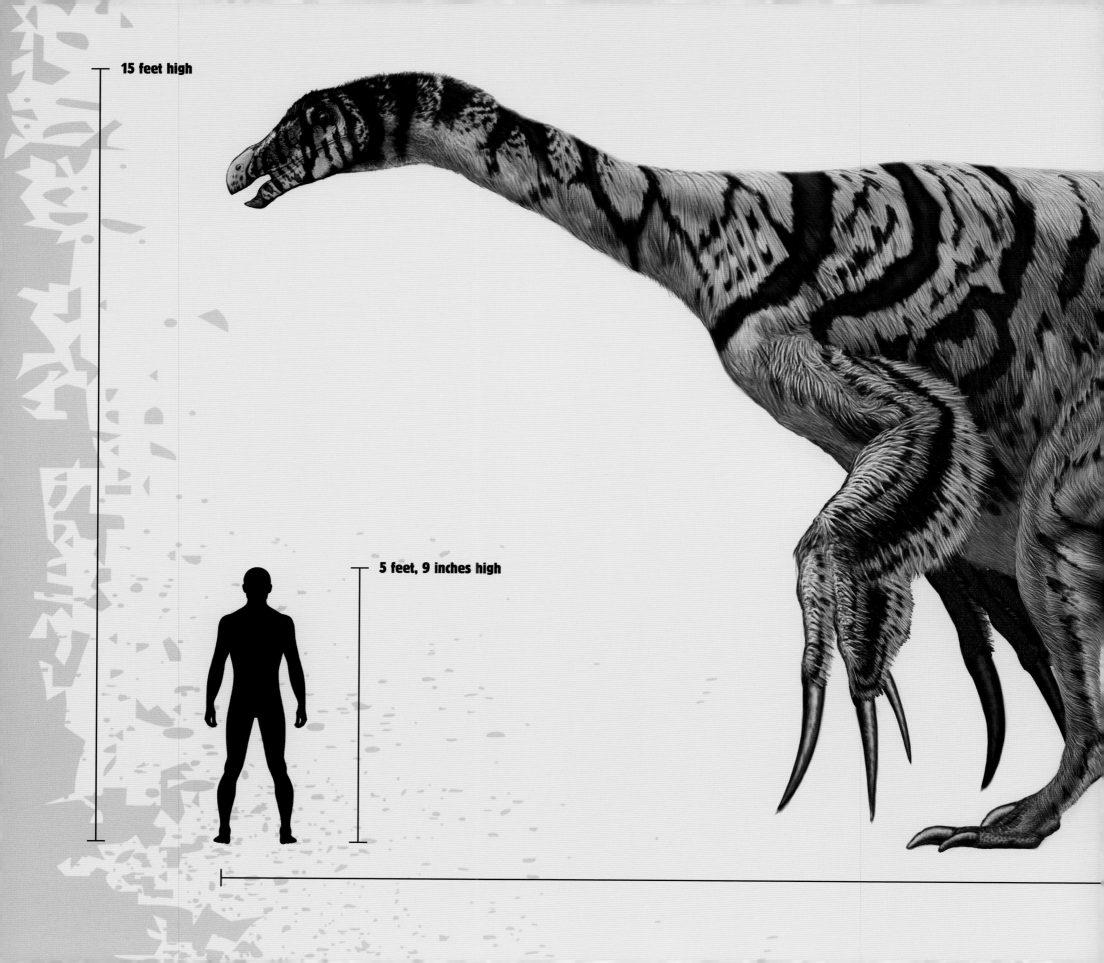

15 feet high

5 feet, 9 inches high

THERIZINOSAURUS
CHELONIFORMIS

PRONUNCIATION: THER-ih-ZEE-no-SAWR-us

SIZE: About 33 feet long

AGE: 70 million years ago

PHYSICAL PROFILE: A large, tubby dinosaur with a tiny head, long neck, and 10-foot-long arms tipped with three-foot-long claws as the end.

SCIENCE BITE: Despite how scary its claws were, *Therizinosaurus* was an omnivore, eating plants as well as fish.

33 feet long

QUETZALCOATLUS
NORTHROPI

PRONUNCIATION: KWET-zal-koh-AT-lus

SIZE: A wingspan of up to 36 feet wide and a height as tall as a giraffe

AGE: 68 million years ago

PHYSICAL PROFILE: One of the biggest flying animals ever, with wings made up of skin stretched between the body and extremely long fourth fingers.

SCIENCE BITE: *Quetzalcoatlus* hunted much the way storks do today, stalking small prey—like baby dinosaurs—and plucking them up with its toothless beak.

TYRANNOSAURUS REX

PRONUNCIATION: tye-RAN-uh-SAWR-us

SIZE: Up to 40 feet long and 9 tons

AGE: 68 to 66 million years ago

PHYSICAL PROFILE: A gigantic carnivore with a large, deep skull and comparatively tiny, two-fingered arms.

SCIENCE BITE: *Tyrannosaurus* wouldn't pass up a free meal, even when it was a member of its own species. Some *Tyrannosaurus* skeletons show bite marks that could only have been caused by other *Tyrannosaurus*.

Tyrannosaurus rex *truly was the king of the tyrant dinosaurs. There were carnivores that got to be just as big, and there were stranger dinosaurs, yet* Tyrannosaurus *continues to dominate our imagination as the epitome of prehistoric predators. Our fear and fascination at the sight of the dinosaur's jaws is part of that.* Tyrannosaurus *could ram its serrated, rail-spike-sized teeth into prey with a force of over 12,8000 pounds, easily puncturing flesh and bone. This let* Tyrannosaurus *take down its victims as well as thoroughly consume carcasses, and, from fossilized* Tyrannosaurus *poop with bone and muscle inside, we know it really did swallow great mouthfuls of flesh. But the jaw muscles were only part of where the predator's power came from.*

The neck muscles of Tyrannosaurus were exceptionally strong. Not only did they allow Tyrannosaurus to kill prey with a side-to-side shake of its head, but, as paleontologists know from bitten bones, they allowed the dinosaur to carefully dismantle carcasses of Triceratops (right). More than that, paleontologists have calculated that Tyrannosaurus had neck muscles strong enough to throw a 110-pound chunk of meat 15 feet into the air and catch it again. To a Tyrannosaurus, you'd be just a quick bite.

CENOZOIC

ERA

66 MILLION YEARS AGO-PRESENT

The very first mammals evolved at about the same time as the first dinosaurs, way back in the Triassic period. For more than 150 million years they coexisted with the "ruling reptiles," evolving into a variety of forms that included beasts similar to flying squirrels, beavers, aardvarks, squirrels, and other mammals familiar to us today. They never got very big. The largest mammal in the Age of Dinosaurs was about the size of a badger. But with the non-avian dinosaurs gone, mammals—as well as other varieties of life—were finally able to evolve into larger, stranger, and more fearsome forms.

All these Cenozoic carnivores are extinct. Yet we still live in an age of impressive hunters. The wolves of the west, the lions of the savanna, the great white sharks in the sea, and even your pet cat—they're all modern carnivores that are carrying on a very old predatory tradition. From the Permian to the present, carnivores have inhabited our world and will continue to stalk our planet far into the future.

ATRACTOSTEUS STRAUSI

PRONUNCIATION: AT-rack-TOE-stee-us

SIZE: Up to 7 feet long

AGE: Eocene, about 50 million years ago

PHYSICAL PROFILE: A large gar, much like those alive today, covered in large scales and with needle-like teeth.

SCIENCE BITE: Paleontologists know a great deal about what *Atractosteus* looked like because of exquisitely preserved fossils from prehistoric lakes that include the scales in place.

Some Cenozoic mammals went through major changes. Starting around 55 million years ago, in the area around present-day India and Egypt, the ancestors of whales started to walk into the ocean. They started out as hoofed mammals that swam in the lakes and rivers of their time, and, in time, their generations became increasingly adapted to life in the water. These "walking whales" were like huge otters with long, sharp-toothed jaws, perfect for snatching fish and even dragging unsuspecting prey into the water. By about 40 million years ago, the walking whales had given rise to ones that lived entirely at sea, like *Dorudon*. The legs sticking out from the sides of *Dorudon* connect them to their amphibious ancestors. And, in time, the descendants of these early whales would become prey themselves. From tooth marks on bones, paleontologists know that *Carcharocles megalodon*—the largest shark that ever lived—frequently fed on blubbery whales.

DORUDON ATROX

PRONUNCIATION: DORR-oo-DON

SIZE: About 16 feet long

AGE: Eocene, 40.4 to 33.9 million years ago

PHYSICAL PROFILE: An early whale with pointed, grabbing teeth at the front of the jaw and shearing teeth in the cheek.

SCIENCE BITE: Baby *Dorudon* had to watch out for bigger whales. Bite marks on one young *Dorudon* skull show it was killed by something bigger, possibly another early whale named *Basilosaurus*.

CARCHAROCLES MEGALODON

PRONUNCIATION: CAR-CHAR-oh-clays

SIZE: Up to 52 feet long and 65 tons

AGE: Oligocene to Pliocene, 28 to 4 million years ago

PHYSICAL PROFILE: The largest shark of all time, similar in form to today's great whites but with more finely serrated teeth.

SCIENCE BITE: Large *C. megalodon* had a bite force of over 41,000 pounds, more than three times that of a *Tyrannosaurus rex*!

Of all the sharks to ever swim the seas, Carcharocles megalodon *was the biggest. And it was also quite long-lived. This 50-foot-long carnivore dined on whales and seals for 14 million years. And maybe, if fossil elephants like this* Platybelodon *swam like some modern elephants do, the shark added pachyderm to its diet, too. We don't have to worry about any of these giants showing up at the beach today, though. The fossil record shows that the enormous shark went extinct about 2 million years ago, long before our species evolved.*

45-million-year-old Megalodon shark tooth.

HYAENODON GIGAS

PRONUNCIATION: HIGH-ay-NO-don

SIZE: Up to the size of a bear

AGE: Eocene to Miocene, 42 to 15.9 million years ago

PHYSICAL PROFILE: A four-legged mammal with piercing teeth at the front of the jaw and cheek teeth that slid past each other to maintain a sharp cutting edge.

Mammals that lived on land took on strange shapes, too. Among the earliest major predators were the creodonts—carnivores like *Hyaenodon* that ran on all fours and sheared through flesh with specialized cheek teeth that slid past each other to always give them a sharp cutting edge. And *Hyaenodon* (left) had competition. It lived alongside other carnivores such as *Archaeotherium* (middle), a "hell pig" with nightmarishly large jaws, and *Dinictis* (right), a cat-like sabertooth that belonged to an extinct group of predators called nimravids. All these Cenozoic predators proliferated in a time before modern groups of carnivores—bears, dogs, cats, and hyenas—replaced them.

DINICTIS
FELINA

PRONUNCIATION: DY-nick-TIS

SIZE: Almost 4 feet long

AGE: Eocene to Miocene, 37.2 to 20.4 million years ago

PHYSICAL PROFILE: A cat-like "false sabertooth" with retractable claws and elongated canines.

ARCHAEOTHERIUM
MORTONI

PRONUNCIATION: AR-kay-o-THEER-ee-um

SIZE: About 7 feet long

AGE: Eocene to Oligocene, 38 to 24.8 million years ago

PHYSICAL PROFILE: A pig-like hoofed mammal with long jaws fitted with piercing, slicing, and crushing teeth.

TITANIS WALLERI

PRONUNCIATION: TIE-tan-ISS

SIZE: About 8 feet tall

AGE: Pliocene, 4.9 to 1.8 million years ago

PHYSICAL PROFILE: A large "terror bird" with small wings, strong legs, and a deep, powerful beak.

SCIENCE BITE: Since birds are dinosaurs, *Titanis* counts as a dinosaurian predator that lived much closer to us in time!

Giant carnivorous birds evolved multiple times during the last 66 million years, and the most impressive of all were the terror birds. These flightless birds first evolved in prehistoric South America about 62 million years ago and were major predators there until 2.5 million years ago; one of the last—*Titanis*—made it to North America before perishing. They evolved a variety of sizes, but the largest were almost 10 feet tall, equipped with sharp talons and strong beaks. These big birds were not friendly.

Even though terror birds evolved in South America, Titanis *did something different:* It traveled north. After tens of millions of years of isolation, South America became connected to North America by the connection with Panama about 7 million years ago. This allowed animals like sabercats and mastodons to travel south, and South American creatures—such as giant sloths and terror birds—to move north. Titanis *was one of these ancient explorers, and the big bird made it as far as Florida.*

Index

About the Author

Brian Switek is a science writer and fossil fanatic. In addition to his books for adults—*Written in Stone* and *My Beloved Brontosaurus*—he blogs for *National Geographic*, hosts the short film series "Dinologue," and volunteers with museums and universities to discover new fossils across the American West. He lives in Utah.

About the Illustrator

Julius Csotonyi is one of the world's most high-profile and talented contemporary paleoartists. His considerable academic expertise informs his stunning, dynamic art. He has created life-sized dinosaur murals for the Royal Ontario Museum and for the Dinosaur Hall at the Natural History Museum of Los Angeles County as well as most of the artwork for the new Hall of Paleontology at the Houston Museum of Natural Science. He lives in Canada.

About Applesauce Press
What kid doesn't love Applesauce!

Good ideas ripen with time. From seed to harvest, Applesauce Press crafts books with beautiful designs, creative formats, and kid-friendly information on a variety of topics. Like our parent company, Cider Mill Press Book Publishers, our press bears fruit twice a year, publishing a new crop of titles each spring and fall.

"Where Good Books Are Ready for Press"

Visit us on the web at
www.cidermillpress.com
or write to us at
PO Box 454
12 Spring Street
Kennebunkport, ME 04046